The New Great Gatsby

Chapter 1: It all starts at the gaming table

Nick Carraway arrives in West Egg, full of ambition and hope that he can find his place in the big world. He rents a small, modest house adjacent to an imposing mansion whose owner he does not yet know. In the evenings, instead of enjoying the peace and quiet or writing letters to his family, he starts visiting a local gambling club with the graceful name Golden Chips.

The club does not smell of sophistication, rather a sultry mix of cigar smoke, cheap coffee and adrenaline. Nick, at first intimidated, is quickly drawn into the atmosphere of the place. That evening he takes a seat at a table where a game of blackjack is being played. His nervous attempts at betting draw the attention of the man sitting across from him - a confident man in a suit with a perfectly knotted tie. The stranger, who introduces himself as Jay Gatsby, looks at Nick with a slight smile.

- "Don't bet on luck, peasant. That will get you lost. You must have a strategy."
- "And what strategy do you propose?" - Nick asks with some embarrassment.

- "One in which you are always one step ahead of the others. Even if you're losing, it's as if you're winning."

The conversation quickly moves beyond the game - Gatsby draws Nick into a fascinating monologue about modern technology, cryptocurrencies and the opportunities afforded by investing in the digital future. Nick, although he completely misunderstands these concepts, feels fascinated. This is the first time anyone has treated him with such enthusiasm.

Gatsby - the mysterious visionary

Jay Gatsby, as it turns out, is a regular at Golden Chips. He has a reputation as a man who always wins - whether at poker or in business. However, no one knows exactly what he does for a living. Some say he made his fortune selling real estate, others say he owns an auction portal. Gatsby does not dispel these rumors. In an interview with Nick, he reveals only that he is "building something big, something that will change the world."

Nick, though skeptical, can't hide his admiration. This man seems to have it all - the confidence, charisma and vision that Nick lacks. What's more, Gatsby offers him something unusual: an invitation to one of his legendary parties at the mansion.

- "Come, Nick. You will see what real life is like. I want you to meet people who are changing the world. Maybe you'll even play a poker final?"

Nick agrees, though he's not sure what awaits him. When he leaves the club late at night, he feels a strange mixture of excitement and anxiety. Who is Jay Gatsby? Why does he seem so interested in a young, average neighbor? And what is so hidden behind his mysterious residence?

The chapter ends as Nick looks at Gatsby's gigantic house, whose windows glow with light and muffled music comes from the distance. This is no ordinary mansion. It's a place where something Nick will remember for the rest of his life may be starting - though he doesn't yet know whether it will be the beginning of happiness or disaster.

Chapter 2: Daisy's dream and cryptocurrency investments

Nick visits Gatsby's mansion for the first time, invited after the events at the gambling club. The vastness of the mansion stuns him - gleaming marble floors, walls filled with screens showing stock market quotes, and soft music from a gramophone in the background. In one room, Gatsby runs what appears to be a small "cryptocurrency exchange." - a group of people clicking fiercely on laptops, who every now and then erupt in excitement as quotes rise or fall.

Gatsby is sitting at his desk, absorbed in his work, but when he notices Nick, he invites him to his personal office. It is there that the words are spoken that will change the course of their acquaintance.

Gatsby and his dream of Daisy

Gatsby lowers his voice, as if afraid that someone will hear:

- "Nick, I have to tell you something. Everything I do, every step, every dollar, every investment.... it's all for her. For Daisy."

Before Nick has time to ask who Daisy is, Gatsby unfolds his story. He tells of his youthful love for Daisy Buchanan, a woman who was everything to him - the epitome of beauty, elegance and wealth he never had. Daisy, who came from a wealthy family, married Tom Buchanan when Gatsby was still a poor penniless soldier.

- "I can't get her back if I'm just rich. I have to be someone. Someone who has created something that will change the world. Someone who has earned his name."

That's why his new project was created - a cryptocurrency called GatsbyCoin.

Birth of GatsbyCoin

Gatsby proudly explains his plan to Nick. GatsbyCoin is to be more than a currency - it is to become a symbol of luxury and aspiration, something that every rich person on the

East Coast will want to own. Gatsby reveals that he has already managed to convince several influential people to invest in the project.

Nick is intrigued, but also concerned. He doesn't understand the world of cryptocurrencies, and he himself has financial problems that he hides from Gatsby. After a while, Gatsby gets to the point:

- "I need someone I can trust, Nick. I want you to help me develop GatsbyCoin. In return ... I will make you a rich man."

Nick, despite his inner reluctance, agrees. He is too caught up in Gatsby's charisma and passion to refuse. But instead of getting on with the project right away, he starts thinking about how to raise money for his first investment.

Nick in trouble

That same evening, Nick visits his family home, which has long stood empty. There, in an act of desperation, he decides to pawn the property to raise money for a share in GatsbyCoin. He feels remorse, but explains to himself that this is a chance for a better life - both for him and his family.

When he returns to Gatsby's residence with documents confirming the investment, Gatsby is waiting for him with a glass of champagne in hand.

- "Welcome to my world, Nick. We are on the threshold of greatness."

The chapter ends with a scene in which Gatsby shows Nick a photo of Daisy in a silver frame standing on his desk. You can see the determination in his eyes - for him, GatsbyCoin is not just a project. It's a bridge to the woman he has never stopped loving. Nick begins to understand that he has entered into something much bigger than any investment.

Chapter 3: Daisy the detective in an evening gown

At the Buchanan estate, an elegant mansion full of marble staircases and crystal chandeliers, Daisy spends the evening in a way no one would expect. Instead of relaxing in the living room, she looks through old maps, notes and photographs of her family, focusing on one detail: a mysterious key-shaped necklace that, according to legend, leads to the family treasure.

Ever since she was a child, Daisy had heard stories about the wealth hidden by her great-great-grandfather, an eccentric millionaire who had a habit of hiding gold coins in the most unexpected places. Until recently, she thought these stories were nonsense, but a certain document found in a family album caught her attention - a sketch of a map that marked a place near... West Egg.

Daisy and her plan

Daisy is convinced that Gatsby's mansion, full of glamour and secrets, may be hiding something more than luxury furniture and partygoers. As Tom engages in his new hobby - organizing arm wrestling competitions in their basement - Daisy begins to hatch a plan.

She doesn't reveal her intentions to anyone, not even her best friend Jordan Baker. During the day she pretends to be a slightly bored upper-class lady, but at night she searches through family records and practices opening locks with a set of picks she bought online.

"If anyone has this treasure, it's Gatsby," thinks Daisy, looking at the mansion across the water. "And if I find it, I'll be free of Tom and his obsession with arm wrestling."

Daisy's first mission

Daisy decides to act. Under the pretext of visiting an old acquaintance in West Egg, she dresses in a dazzling evening gown - long, silk, ivory-colored - and sets off for Gatsby's mansion. Her elegance causes her to be welcomed with open arms by the butler.

On the spot, Daisy attracts the attention of guests and Gatsby himself, who has long dreamed of meeting her. Gatsby, thinking that Daisy visited him because of romantic feelings, immediately starts showing her around his house. He shows her the ballroom, the library and the impressive terrace overlooking the bay.

But Daisy is focused on something else. Her gaze wanders over the walls, floors and decorations, as if looking for hidden passageways or hiding places. When Gatsby leaves for a moment to order a glass of champagne for her, Daisy uses the moment to quickly scan one of the offices. Her search is interrupted by the sound of footsteps - Gatsby is returning.

Tom and his competition

Meanwhile, Tom Buchanan, unaware of his wife's obsession, holds his first big armwrestling tournament in the basement. His goal is to prove that he is still "manly" and dominant, especially amid growing rumors of his affair with Myrtle.

The competition is a big event - among the participants are his friends from the golf club and some local workers he hired to "increase the competition." Tom, dressed in a sports tracksuit, completely ignores the fact that Daisy is not at home.

Back at the mansion

Gatsby finally notices that Daisy is acting strangely. When he asks her if she's okay, Daisy responds with an innocent smile:

- "Oh, Jay, I'm just impressed.... this place. I've always wondered what secrets a house like this holds."

Gatsby interprets this as a romantic remark and begins to talk about his efforts to win her heart, but Daisy listens with one ear. Her thoughts revolve around the treasure - could it be hidden in the basement? Or perhaps in one of the ornate columns?

The chapter ends with Daisy returning home, slightly disappointed, but even more determined. She already has a plan for her next visit - this time she intends to find a way to get into the less public parts of the mansion. She has no intention of letting go, especially since the treasure could be her key to a new life.

Chapter 4: Cryptocurrency ball and drone festival

There's a strange sound above Gatsby's residence that attracts the attention of West Egg residents. It's not the jazz everyone has grown accustomed to, but a distinctive buzzing sound - the sound of dozens of drones circling over the property. That evening, Gatsby is hosting an event that will forever change the definition of elegance in West Egg.

Welcome to the world of the future

Gatsby's residence looks like a futuristic conference center. Instead of champagne-filled fountains, guests are greeted by huge LED screens displaying stock market charts and dynamic animations depicting GatsbyCoin. Serving robots roam around the garden, delivering cocktails and avocado sandwiches, and a drone show takes place in the main courtyard, with lights spinning in the sky to create captions like: "The financial revolution begins here!"

Nick, who is involved in organizing the event, is watching it all with a mixture of awe and anxiety. Gatsby is in his element, welcoming investors, startups and tech influencers who have come from all over the coast. Nick notes, however, that the whole event is more cold and calculating than previous lavish parties - no live music, carefree dancing or candid conversations.

Daisy takes the stage

Daisy arrives late in the evening, dressed in a classic pearl gown that contrasts with the futuristic decor of the party. Gatsby, as soon as he spots her, immediately drops everything to greet her. There is the same determination in his eyes as always - this is the moment to impress the woman of his life.

However, Daisy, enthralled at first by the drone show, soon begins to feel out of place. Trying to engage her in conversation, Gatsby leads her to the main stage, where a crowd of attendees is waiting for a presentation of his project. Daisy doesn't understand why, instead of a quiet, romantic meeting, Gatsby has chosen an evening full of numbers, charts and technological presentations.

- "Jay, what does all this mean?" - asks Daisy, seeing Gatsby preparing for his speech.

- "Daisy, this is the future. This is what will show you that I'm worth more than Tom. You'll see."

GatsbyCoin - a "pitch" without love

On stage, Gatsby enthusiastically talks about his project: how GatsbyCoin will change the way people think about investing and become a symbol of luxury for a new generation. The presentation is professional, full of impressive animations and catchy slogans, but Daisy looks on with a mixture of amazement and disappointment.

- "Is he just trying to seduce me.... cryptocurrency?" - he thinks, glancing at Gatsby, who gestures passionately as he explains the intricacies of blockchain.

Daisy is beginning to long for the old days, when romance didn't require technology and men competed for her attention with a bouquet of flowers rather than graphics from a projector.

Tom and his surprising proposal

Meanwhile, Tom Buchanan, who is finally beginning to suspect something about Daisy and Gatsby's intimacy, decides to attend the event in person. Entering, he feels like a fish out of water - people dressed in designer clothes, talking about tokens and startups, this is not his world. Nevertheless, he quickly tracks down Daisy and Gatsby, who are standing in a corner after the presentation.

- "So this is what these business meetings of yours are like?" - chuckles Tom, glancing at Gatsby.

Rather than getting into a confrontation, Gatsby starts talking about the potential of GatsbyCoin as an investment. Tom, to the surprise of both Gatsby and Daisy, does not get angry, but begins to inquire about the details.

- "Wait, wait... you say you can earn 200% in a month? Why not give it a try? I have a few friends who might be interested in it."

Daisy, watching this absurd conversation, feels everything she has known begin to crumble. The man who loved her without boundaries now sees her as nothing more than an excuse to pursue his obsession, and her husband, who had always ignored her, suddenly took an interest in the world he had previously ridiculed.

Daisy quits

The party is in full swing, but Daisy has had enough. On the pretext of being tired, she leaves the mansion, leaving Gatsby and Tom in a heated discussion about the potential of cryptocurrencies. When she returns to her residence, she feels a strange emptiness. Does either of the two men really understand her?

The chapter ends with an image of Gatsby, standing on the balcony of his house, staring at the disappearing lights of Daisy's car. There is still hope smoldering in his eyes - though now perhaps more for GatsbyCoin than for love.

Chapter 5: Escape from West Egg

Everything in West Egg is beginning to fall apart, and the semblance of success and luxury that surrounded Gatsby is slowly giving way to a reality full of deception, tension and desperation.

Nick and a risky attempt on the black market

Nick, more depressed with each passing day, finds himself in a no-win situation. He invested everything he had - and even what he didn't have - in GatsbyCoin, which is now proving unstable. Its value is dropping day by day, and Nick sees that the project is not as solid as Gatsby had convinced him.

Determined to get at least some of his money back, Nick makes contact with a cryptocurrency trader on the black market in New York. It's a suspicious meeting in a dingy warehouse with flickering light bulbs and thin walls instead of luxury. The trader, a man with a nervous look and restless movements, doesn't have good news:

- "GatsbyCoin? Dude, it's practically a meme now. But I can give you something.... For half the market price."

Nick, knowing he has no choice, accepts the terms. But his desperation attracts attention, and barely out of the warehouse, he notices he's being followed. On his way back to West Egg, he feels that he has fallen into something much bigger than he can imagine.

Daisy discovers the truth

Daisy, increasingly determined to solve the mystery of the "treasures" in Gatsby's mansion, decides to make a final search. She chooses the moment when Gatsby is holding a meeting with another group of investors. With flashlight in hand, she searches the less frequented parts of the mansion - the basement, attic and secret locked rooms.

What she discovers is not the treasure she expected. Instead of gold coins and precious jewels, Daisy finds piles of documents - fake contracts, unrealized projects and plans that never had a chance to succeed. GatsbyCoin, it turns out, was just an illusion - another attempt by Gatsby to create something great and impress her.

When Gatsby finds her, Daisy is standing in his office, holding one of his advertising flyers.

- "It's all a lie, isn't it?" - he says with coldness in his voice.

- "Daisy, you haven't understood. I'm doing all this for us. It's not about money, but about love. About you."

Gatsby, in an attempt to regain control, convinces Daisy that "love is the greatest treasure," and that everything he did was to win her heart. But for Daisy, his words are already empty.

Dramatic ending

Daisy leaves without looking back. In her haste, closing the door behind her, she accidentally destroys Gatsby's favorite drone - a small gold DJI with "The Sky's the Limit" engraved on it. The drone, a symbol of Gatsby's ambitions and dreams, crashes to the floor.

A distraught Gatsby tries to stop her, but Daisy is adamant. She gets into her car and drives off into the night, leaving behind a world full of false promises.

Nick and the fall

Nick returns to Gatsby's residence at the same time as Daisy leaves. He sees Gatsby standing at the entrance, holding a damaged drone, with an expression of emptiness in his eyes.

- "I lost everything, Nick. Her ... And what I wanted to build."

Nick doesn't know what to answer. Sam feels at a loss - with debts, fraud and the uncertainty of what the future will bring. The chapter ends with the two men standing silently in front of the mansion, looking at the dark sky, where no drones are flying around anymore.

LED screens flash in the background, displaying the latest GatsbyCoin quotes: down 90%.

Chapter 6: The supermarket accident

After escaping from Gatsby's mansion, Daisy can't find peace. Her idealistic dreams of finding the treasure that would be the key to a new life are crumbling like a china cup. Filled with frustration and a sense of aimlessness, she decides to go about her daily business - including shopping at the local supermarket.

Trouble between the shelves

The supermarket in West Egg is a place where luxurious marble floors contrast strangely with cheap shopping carts. Daisy, dressed in an elegant coat and pearl jewelry, definitely stands out among the customers. She begins to fill her cart, trying to occupy her thoughts with something mundane - a choice between organic and vegan milk.

But the tension within her is mounting. When a young mother appears in the alley and accidentally gets in her way, Daisy shoots her an icy stare, then violently pushes her stroller. Unfortunately, by unfortunate coincidence, the stroller hits an exposed stack of milk and egg cartons.

The domino effect is immediate. Milk spills onto the floor, eggs shatter in spectacular chaos. Customers look on in surprise, and supermarket employees begin to gather mops and buckets. Daisy stands still, stunned, trying to understand what has just happened.

Myrtle enters the scene

At this point Myrtle, who works as a cashier at the same supermarket, appears. Myrtle, who has long secretly dreamed of breaking out of the monotony of her life, recognizes Daisy and sees an opportunity for some form of cooperation.

- "Don't worry, Mrs. Buchanan. We can settle this quietly." - Myrtle says, leaning in conspiratorially.

- "I know a few tricks that can make sure no one notices the damage."

Daisy, despite her initial surprise, quickly agrees to Myrtle's plan. Her frustration begins to turn into a certain excitement - an unusual plot with a complete stranger almost seems like a form of revenge against the world that has failed her.

Myrtle's plan

Myrtle proposes to distract the store manager and customers. Together they create a chaotic staging: Myrtle deliberately knocks down a shelf of chips, while Daisy leads the cart away from the scene of the accident, pretending that nothing happened. The plan is absurd and full of loopholes, but it works.

"I never thought I could do something like this," - Daisy thinks, hiding a smile.

"Maybe I have something of the rebel in me after all."

After everything, Myrtle gives Daisy a meaningful look that says: "You owe me something for this." Daisy, to her surprise, feels a strange gratitude toward the woman she previously thought of as a mere working-class girl.

Tom and a new obsession

Meanwhile, Tom Buchanan, completely oblivious to his wife's little crisis, is busy with his new passion - his career as a fitness influencer. Ever since someone offered him the chance to collaborate on a dietary supplement commercial, Tom felt he had finally found a way to gain publicity and recognition.

In the living room of their mansion, Tom makes videos in which he shows off his perfectly sculpted biceps and talks about "inner strength." He doesn't even notice when Daisy comes home - all emotional after her adventure in the supermarket.

- "If your life seems chaotic, remember that only discipline and protein can restore balance!" - says Tom to the camera, while Daisy walks past him with a sarcastic smile.

End of the day

Sitting in her room late at night, Daisy recalls the events at the supermarket. For the first time in a long time, she feels that she did something spontaneously and on her own - even if it was absurd. But the realization that her life is still full of emptiness comes back like a boomerang.

On the first floor, Tom's voice can be heard talking on the phone about his plans to work with another fitness sponsor. Daisy realizes that neither he, nor Gatsby, nor anyone else cares about her real needs or dreams.

The chapter ends with an image of Daisy looking out the window at the dark streets of West Egg, in a reverie about the next step she could take to find herself in all this.

Chapter 7: The end of dreams, the beginning of new startups

Silence falls in West Egg, where dreams and ambitions once seemed to grow faster than real estate prices. A chapter full of losses, resurgent aspirations and new beginnings shows that life, even after a fall, can find a new form - though not always the one expected.

Gatsby and the NFT - the last hope

Jay Gatsby sits alone in his mansion, surrounded by mementos of the old days - party photos, empty champagne bottles and unfinished GatsbyCoin projects. After the collapse of his cryptocurrency and his failure to win Daisy's heart, Gatsby is a shadow of his former self.

However, as always, his steadfast optimism finds a way to rebuild. One night, while browsing the Internet for inspiration, he comes across a hot topic - NFT (Non-Fungible Tokens).

- "This is it. A new opportunity, a new market. When everyone sees ruins, I see gold."

Gatsby decides to create a series of NFTs depicting iconic moments from his life - his famous suit, his mansion, and even a drone with the words "The Sky's the Limit." The idea seems absurd, but Gatsby believes he can once again become a leader in the world of modern technology.

Nick - back to his roots

Nick Carraway, tired of the chaos and devastated by his debts, decides to abandon West Egg and return to his family home in the Midwest. Unfortunately, he discovers that his home has been sold by a bank for a fraction of its value to pay off his outstanding debts.

With a heavy heart, Nick decides to start all over again, away from the toxic reality of the rich and ambitious. He buys a train ticket and sets off on a return trip, taking with him only a suitcase full of memories and a handful of lessons he learned on the East Coast.

- "No more false friends and promises. I'm going back to simplicity. Maybe that's where I'll find myself."

Daisy - a new path

Daisy Buchanan, after years of living in the shadow of men who tried to shape her reality, decides to take matters into her own hands. She opens a detective agency called "Buchanan Investigations," specializing in cases of infidelity, secrets and... treasures.

Her first assignments come faster than she expected - wealthy Long Islanders start entrusting her with their most complicated and spicy cases. Daisy, who was previously seen as beautiful but passive, now becomes a master at uncovering the secrets of others.

- "Who knows mysteries better than me?" - he says with a smile, reviewing a new case involving missing jewelry in East Egg.

Tom and the world of fitness

Tom Buchanan, though initially heartbroken by the breakup of his marriage and his loss of control over Daisy, quickly finds solace in his new role. He becomes an ambassador for a luxury brand of protein nutrients and sportswear.

On social media, Tom is now known as "FitTom," and his motivational videos, in which he shouts at viewers about the importance of self-discipline, are garnering millions of views.

- "If life throws burdens under your feet, pick them up!" - he says in one of the viral clips.

Tom seems to be happy in the role, although his worldview is now strangely simplified: everything comes down to protein and training.

Epilogue

Each character is in a different place - literally and metaphorically. Gatsby is still struggling, trying to be reborn in a world of digital assets. Nick abandons the world of illusion and returns to a simple life. Daisy discovers a new strength within herself, becoming independent and entrepreneurial. And Tom, though still superficial, finds fulfillment in the world of muscle and social media.

West Egg and East Egg remain as beautiful and illusory as ever, but those who have lived there know that they can no longer rely on the illusion of the American Dream. A new chapter of life opens for each of them - though the question still remains whether they will find happiness in it.

Chapter 8: And so we sail... into endless debt

The final chapter is full of quiet, albeit bitter, reckoning between the characters and what they experienced in West Egg. Instead of grand finales, we get a picture of life going on - not necessarily in glory, but with a bit of acceptance of their own failures and absurdities.

Nick and his attempt to embrace finances

Nick Carraway, still crushed by his West Egg experience, finally admits to himself that he lacked one fundamental skill: money management. After returning to the Midwest, he enrolls in an online financial course called "Your Money, Your Rules."

In between video lectures given by an over-enthusiastic financial trainer, Nick reflects on the past: on Gatsby, Daisy, Tom and the whole strange world that has consumed him.

"Maybe the problem wasn't just greed or love of luxury. Maybe it's we humans who tend to complicate things that could be simple."

Nick tries to write his memoirs, but instead of deep reflections, chaotic notes come out. Eventually he puts down his pen, deciding that it might be better to focus on simpler goals - like learning how to budget.

Gatsby - new hope in Silicon Valley

Jay Gatsby, though exhausted and ruined, is not giving up on his dreams. He buys a one-way ticket to California, where he wants to make a fresh start in Silicon Valley. He believes that there, in the heart of technological innovation, he will find an environment more receptive to his ongoing ambitions and dreams of greatness.

During his last conversation with Nick, on the station platform, Gatsby smiles with a mixture of weariness and hope.

- "Don't worry, Nick. You'll hear about Jay Gatsby again. This time it will be different. It's no longer about money or Daisy. It's about the future."

Gatsby disappears into the crowd of travelers, holding a laptop and a bundle of notes full of new start-up ideas.

Daisy and a stable life

Daisy, after a tumultuous period of emotional dramas and failed investigations, finds surprising peace. Her detective agency works well enough to provide her with a stable, if unexciting, life. In the evenings, she sits in her office, reviews case files and sips tea.

Tom Buchanan, who now leads her career as a fitness influencer, occasionally visits her with their daughter. Their relationship is cool but pragmatic - no great emotions, no conflict. Daisy, for the first time in a long time, seems reconciled to this.

Tom and his fitness utopia

Tom Buchanan is finding his place in the fitness world. His Instagram account reaches a million followers, and slogans such as "There are no excuses, only weights" and "Protein above everything" are becoming his calling card.

Tom has been making increasingly bizarre videos - like the one where he picks up the refrigerator as part of a challenge, or offers a 30-day "everything from eggs" challenge. His life is strangely stable, though lacking in depth.

The finale - the last $2

The novel ends with a scene that is a sad but telling symbol of Nick's situation. After a lecture on finance, Nick goes to a small corner store, where he notices a candy bar called "Dream of Caramel."

"It's absurd, but who wouldn't want a little dream for $2?"

Nick reaches into his wallet and pulls out the last bills, buying a candy bar. He walks down the street, slowly unwrapping the paper, and eats the first bites, wondering if he will ever feel truly fulfilled.

Last words

Nick ends his narrative with a reflection that is strangely simple and human:

"Maybe it's not about flowing to big goals. Maybe life is just a series of small steps... and sometimes a candy bar for the last two dollars."

www.ingramcontent.com/pod-product-compliance
Lightning Source LLC
Chambersburg PA
CBHW070959240526
45469CB00017B/2538